The SINNER & the SAINT

A Book of Poems, Short Stories & Photographs

TRACY CHABRIER

The Sinner & the Saint
A Book of Poems, Short Stories & Photographs
All Rights Reserved.
Copyright © 2022 Tracy Chabrier
v2.0

This is a work of poeticized fiction. The opinions expressed in this manuscript are solely the opinions of the author and do not represent the opinions or thoughts of the publisher. The author has represented and warranted full ownership and/or legal right to publish all the materials in this book.

This book may not be reproduced, transmitted, or stored in whole or in part by any means, including graphic, electronic, or mechanical without the express written consent of the publisher except in the case of brief quotations embodied in critical articles and reviews.

Outskirts Press, Inc.
http://www.outskirtspress.com

Paperback ISBN: 978-1-9772-4777-3

Cover Photo © 2022 Tracy Chabrier. All rights reserved - used with permission.

Outskirts Press and the "OP" logo are trademarks belonging to Outskirts Press, Inc.

PRINTED IN THE UNITED STATES OF AMERICA

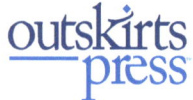

Table of Contents

Foreword .... *i*

A Letter from Santa *1*

Did You Know? *5*

You Cared *7*

The Man from Middletown *9*

This Little Light of Mine *11*

Did I Ever Think? *13*

Drummer Boy *15*

It's Late at Night *17*

Is There Still A Chance? *19*

If You Could See Me Now *21*

My Burning Eyes *23*

You Have Made Me A Writer *25*

Proud and Prolific *27*

When You Love a Phantom *29*

Foreword

Many years ago, while visiting New Orleans with a girlfriend, I had a session with a fortuneteller. She read my palm, and as she did so she gasped. "Oh my!" exclaimed she. "Look at all those lines running through your love-line. You will suffer many heartbreaks in your lifetime, but also, your true love will return to you."

Just recently I was told that Scorpios should never marry.

I have loved several men in my lifetime; and have suffered just as many heartbreaks.

   -TC

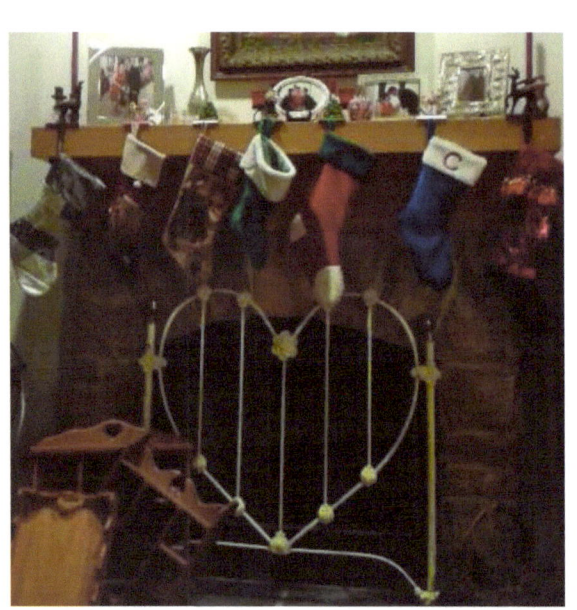

A Letter from Santa

December 2012

My dearest Jacob,

 Firstly, I would like you to know that it was a battle of wills with your mother to convince her to let me bring you this door. I had to explain that a gift is not earned but is given freely of the heart. So that while you may not deserve the door, I have seen that it is your utmost desire. Therefore, I did not give in to her argument, and I am at very last your champion. (No easy task I assure you as she is very clever!!) Let it be known, that just because I have presented it to you does not mean that the door could not be taken away yet again. I am sure you have heard the adage "third time's the charm?" You are old enough now to really understand consequences, eh my boy? I know that you are on the cusp of not really believing any more, but I do think you can still hear the jingle of the silver bells, however faintly… This may be the last time I am able to visit you. I will remember you always as having a good heart. You are in my "Book of Good Boys & Girls." I know you will think of me again years from now when you have had your own children. I have EVERY CONFIDENCE in you, and it is my greatest hope that you will turn out to be a responsible adult. By the way, congratulations on achieving Employee of the Month status. Keep working very hard! Your mother and I are very proud of your work ethic!

 The best gift I could ask in return, if I may, (and I surely know this is unprecedented) is that you think of your mother fondly. While you may not know the sacrifices a single momma makes for her children, she has always had your best interests at the very core of her heart. She raised you and your brother on her own for many, many years always doing her best. Your grandparents did a wonderful job *raising her, and she used those lessons they taught her well. I know it has been a chore for you to read this letter. Thank you for honoring me by taking your time and giving it your best. I won't keep you any longer, as I know you have got some hinge pins with your name on them.*

With all the love this old guy has got,

Santa Claus

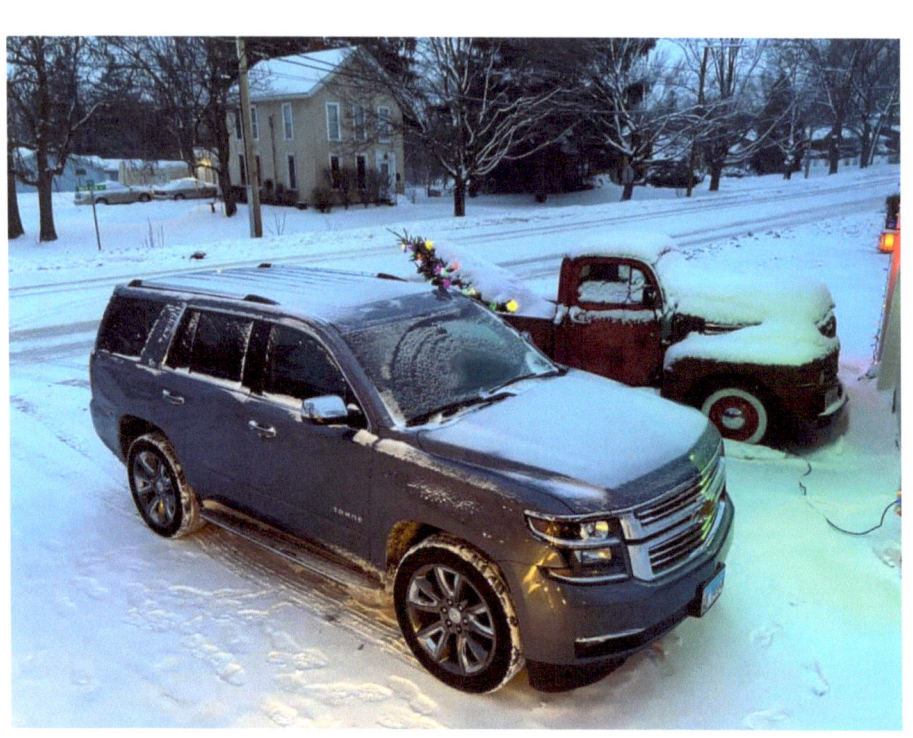

Did You Know?

Did you know when you woke that day, that we'd meet quite by chance?

Did you know that I wouldn't have bought that tank if it weren't for you, but I'm glad that I did?

Did you know that you would make the sun shine for me, on such a gloomy day?

Did you know that you'd catch my eye, and that I'd fall in love?

Did you know that you were gonna break my heart, or did you give it a second thought?

Did you know that my life would never be the same again, since you walked into it?

Did you know that you'd steal my heart, and make my aura dim?

Did you know that I'd like to hold you tonight, but the chance of that is slim?

Did you know when you woke that day, that you would be my sin?

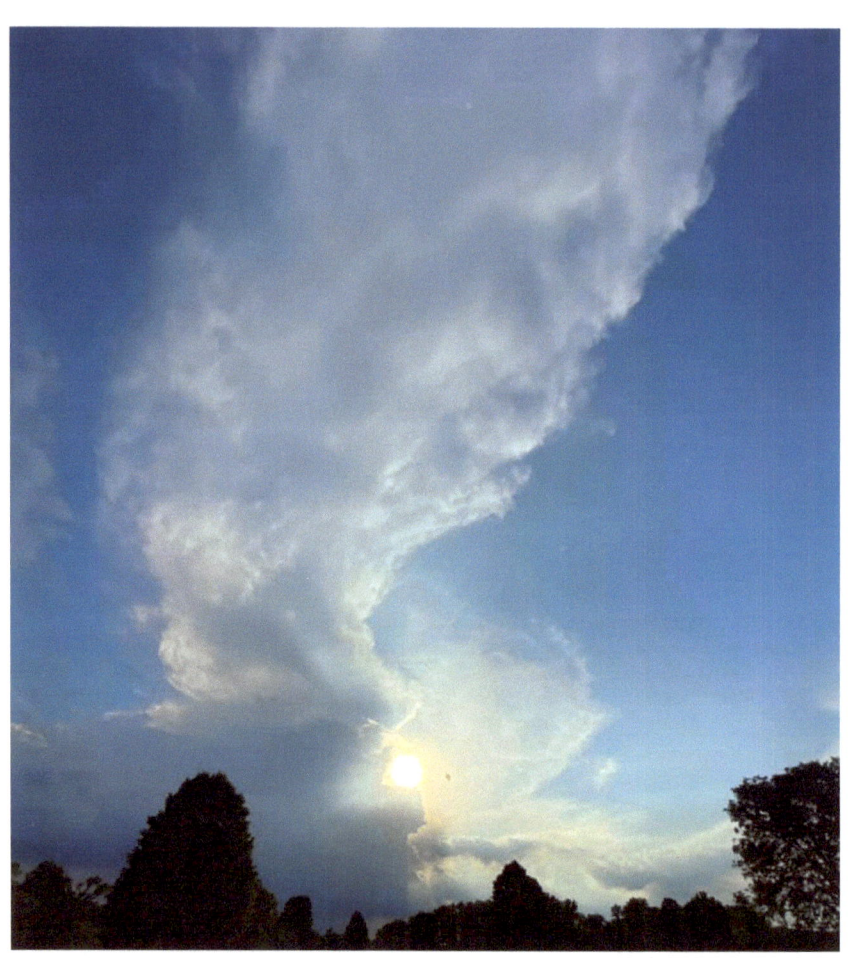

You Cared

You cared about me from the first moment we met. You wanted to hold me, but it was I who asked you for a hug, and you thought I could read your mind.

You cared for me so much that you lead a team to find the best just for me. You would settle for nothing less. You asked for me alone. The spark of a new plan left to fizzle.

Sleepless nights. Thoughts barreling down the tracks of our future, unrealized. Here in an instant unimagined, not having been planned. Innocence. Now gone.

My thoughts of you, reciprocated for me! A chance meeting or fate? Can't get you out of my mind.

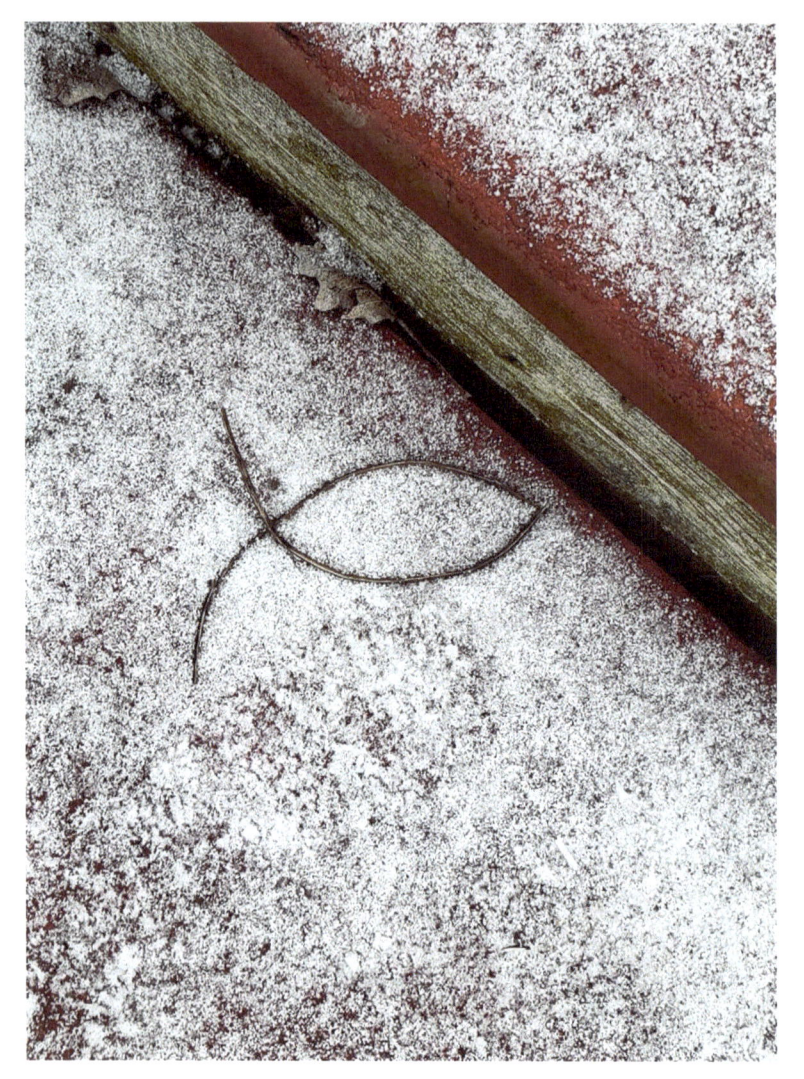

The Man from Middletown

The sun shone through the clouds for a moment in time, but that meant that hope was truly alive.

A look, a touch, the stolen scent of my hair, while you held me in your arms. Eyes that met in the very center of our souls.

And when the butterflies of nerves were gone, and the sad emptiness returned, only the joy of singing worship and praise could right the wrong that never had a chance.

The attraction and the appreciation shared. The excitement of something new. The guilt. The reassurance of nary a thought gone bad. The silence. The pain. The cynical laugh at the bitter taste of truth through the tears.

Only to remember the promise, that He alone has plans for us better than we could ever imagine for ourselves.

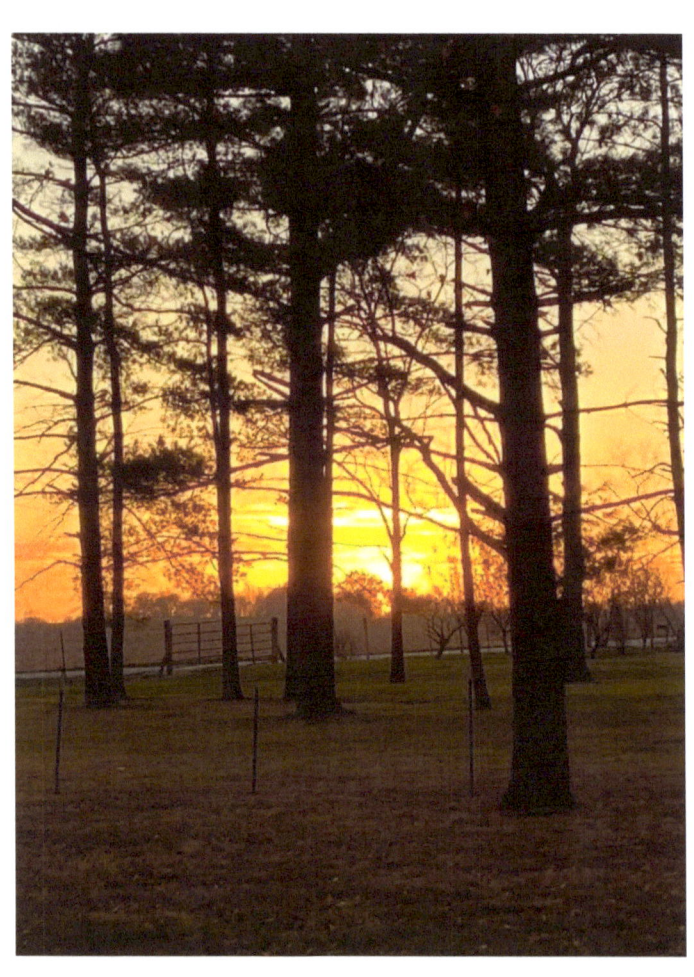

This Little Light of Mine

This little light of mine shines brightly in the dark. It's cold and late, but still I wait, for the screen of my phone to shine.

It was a Friday night when I texted you, just to say hello. It had only been one week you see, but I had to, had to know.

That night felt grand while you held my hand, if only in my dreams. Now I confess I am obsessed, waiting for the light to glow.

It's been some time since that phone did shine, I wonder if it'll ever glow again. You had my heart, right from the start. But maybe it's not meant to be.

You're still you, and I'm still me. I guess we'll just have to wait and see.

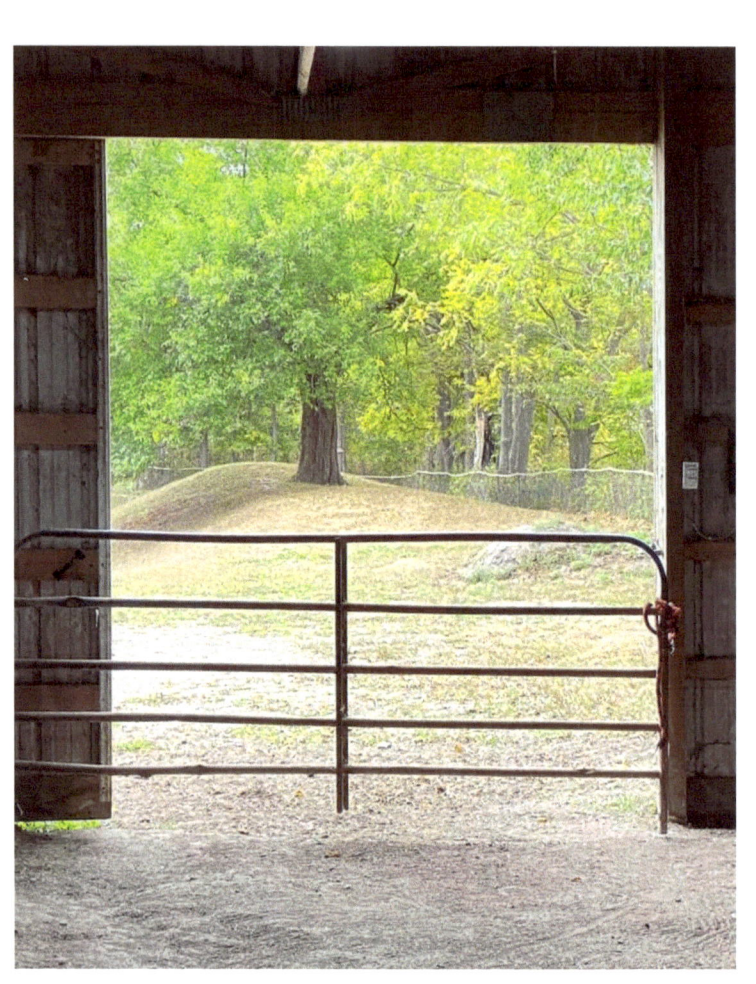

Did I Ever Think?

Did I ever think that I'd leave him blue? Never once till I met you.

I saw you once, and oh how sweet, the thoughts I had of us.

Now you are gone, and here I sit, thinking thoughts of you so blue.

Did I ever think, that once I wanted you, you'd change your mind so quick?

Now I'm thinking, did I ever think, that you could be such a dick? Never once, till I met you!

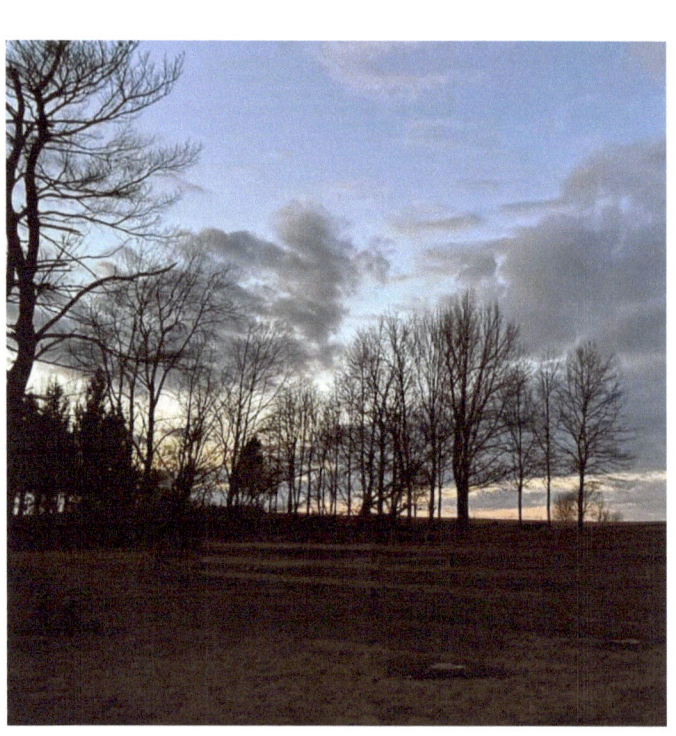

Drummer Boy

Every time I climb into my tank, how can I help but think of you. Your handsome face, your crooked smile. My sweet Prince, Drummer Boy.

The stress of life. The thoughts of nights. My sweet little Drummer Boy.

My sons are grown, but yours needs you now. I'd like to leave, but how? The days are long and miles far, my caring Drummer Boy.

The Queen of the West has held no bounds like the City of Wind could do. You're so far away, but I see you now. I wish you were mine, Drummer Boy.

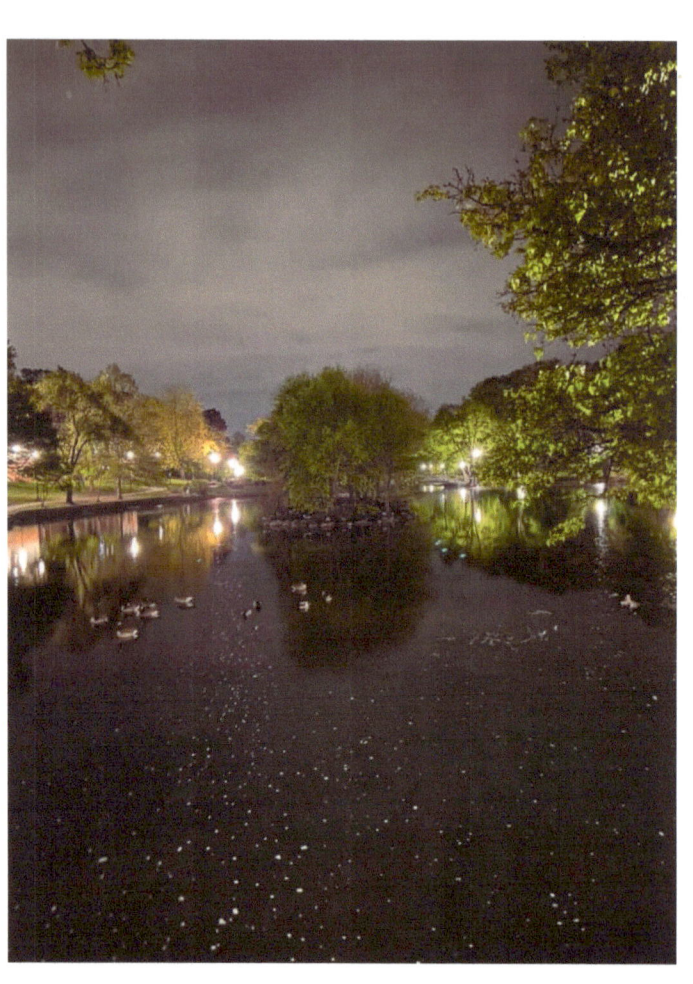

It's Late at Night

It's late at night once again, and here I sit thinking of you. There he lies right next to me snoring up a storm.

I paid twenty bucks to look you up, and you've been verified. It's late at night, once again, and here I sit thinking of you.

Is your boy okay, do you think of me, in these days that have gone by? It's late at night and here I sit, thinking of you bye and bye.

Will I ever see your face again? Here I sit late at night thinking of you once again.

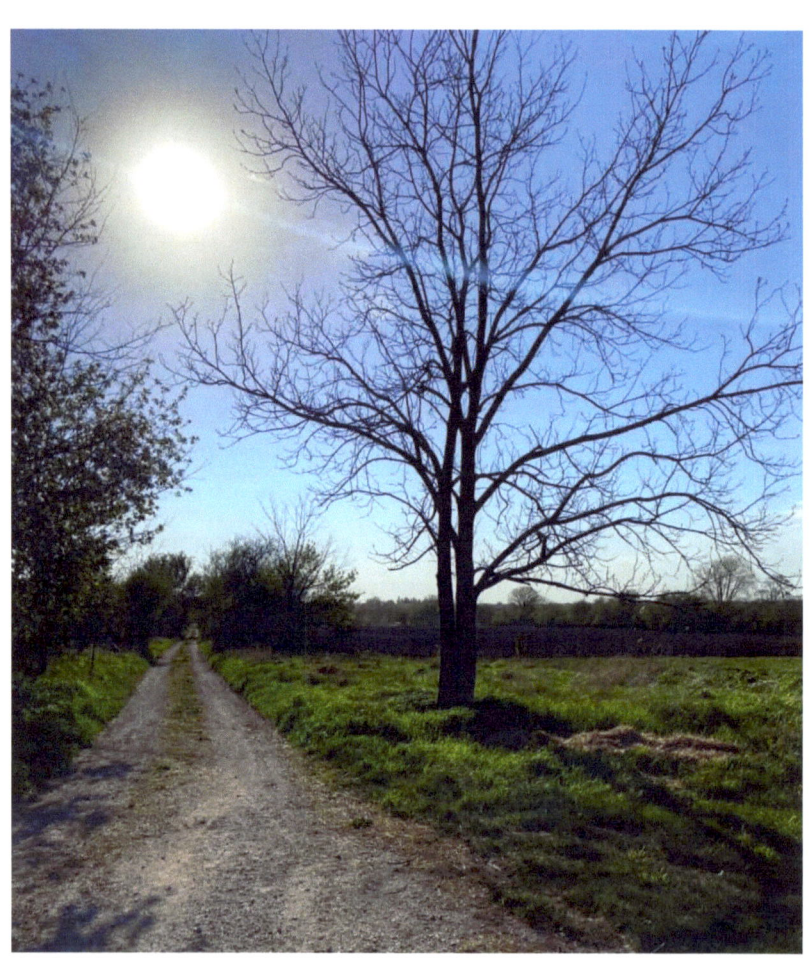

Is There Still A Chance?

Is there still a chance that we could make things work, from here to all the way there? It's a five-hour drive with some dogs in a tank, but I think I'd like to try.

Is there still a chance that your words were true, honest and real? How can I know, in my woe, is there still a chance?

If you won't talk to me, should I think it all was just lies? I need to think in my heart of hearts that there is still a chance!

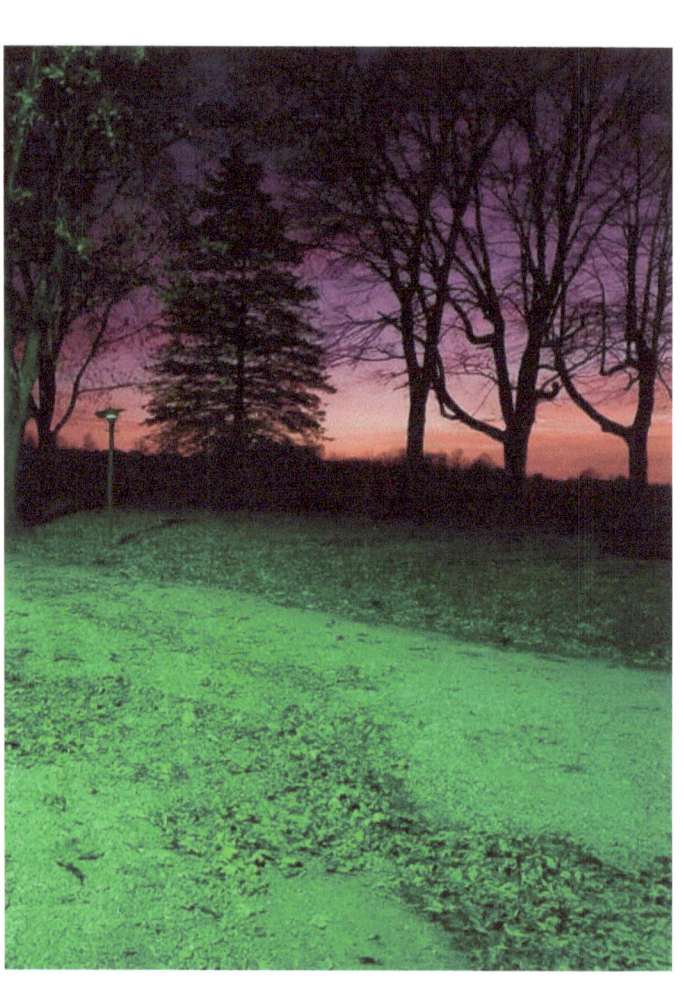

If You Could See Me Now

If you could see me now, I wonder what you'd think. My temper's short and my words are clipped, but how can that be helped?

You wanted me, and I you too, but where are you now? In a hospital room with your fragile boy, not knowing what to do.

I wish I was there, at least for you, but I don't think that's what you want. My tears come quick, with a bitter laugh, how could I be such a fool?

Life is hard, but I have changed. If you could see me now.

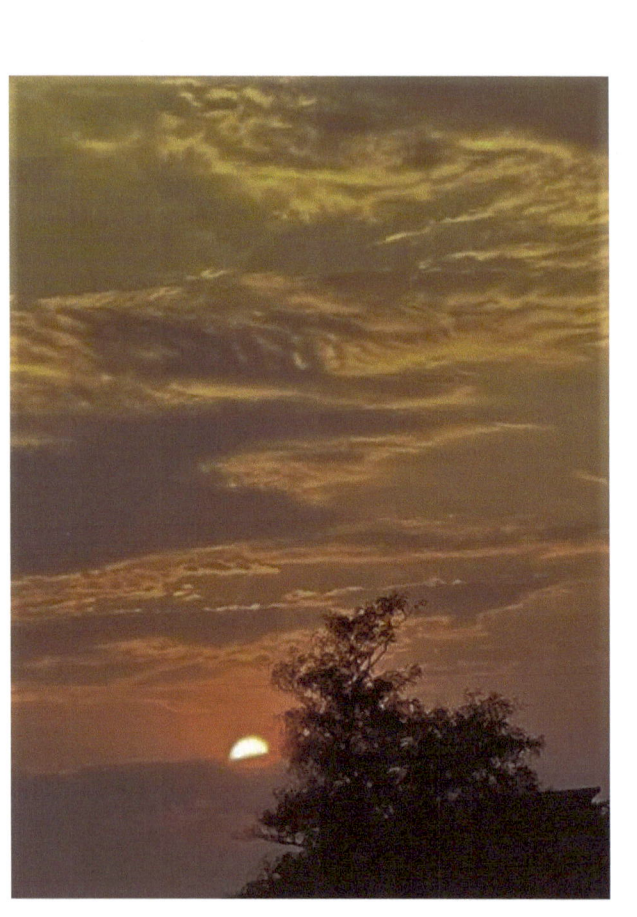

My Burning Eyes

Well, my eyes they are a-burning now because it's late and I've been crying. Are you worth the salt that my tears use up? Well, that is yet to be seen.

My eyes are burning now a glare towards his sleeping head. Do I wish that he was gone, so that I could have made another choice? Maybe, but he's not dead yet.

He tells me every day or so that he's gonna die in his sleep. It's been four years and I'm thinking not, so my eyes are burning.

I think I'm dead, he tells me now, but then what is that I hear? If he were dead, I think I'd know, 'cause he'd stop the constant talking.

My burning eyes they come and go, should I laugh, or should I cry? Well maybe I'll find out some day, and my burning eyes will go away.

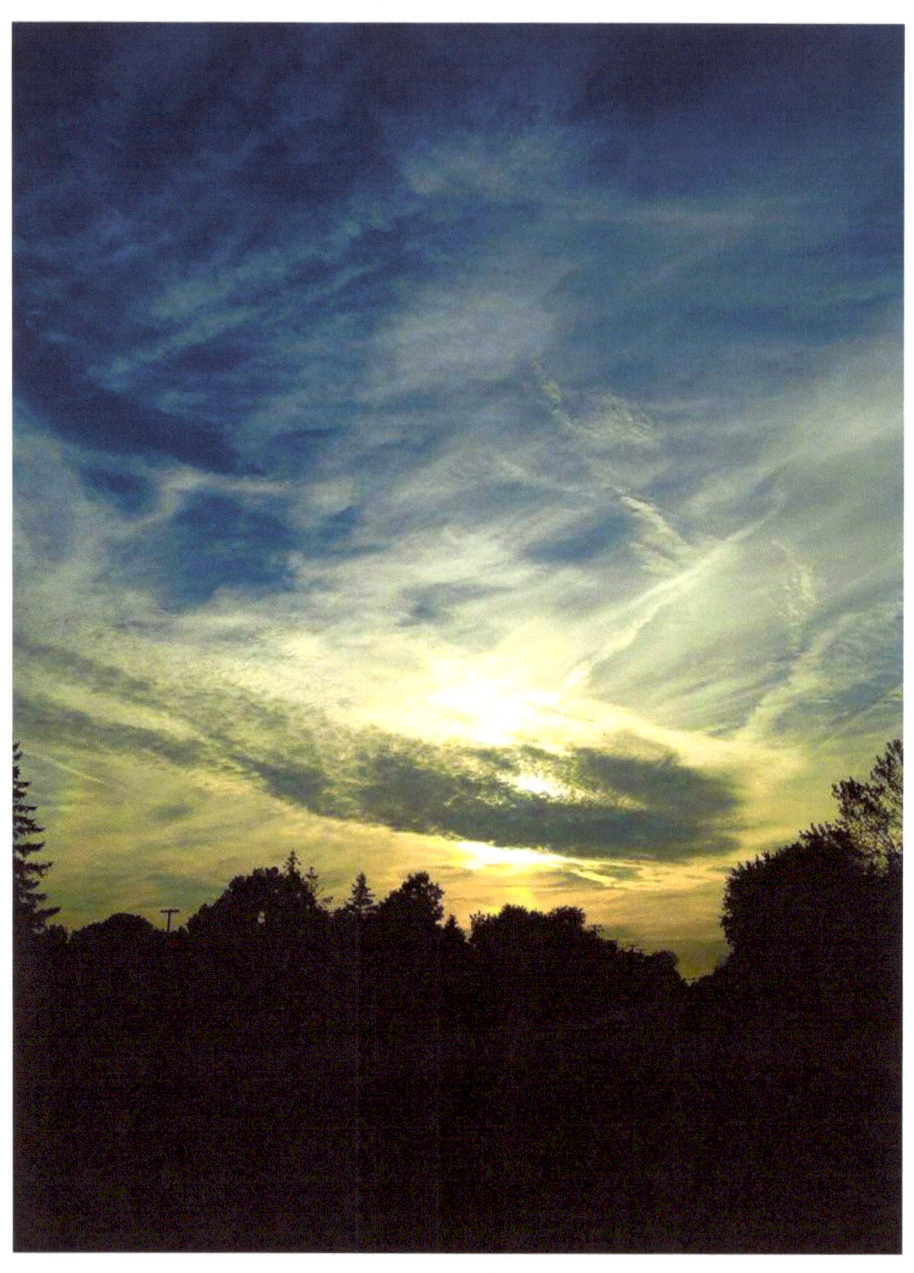

You Have Made Me A Writer

I always have wanted to write, a poem now and then. A novel I did start to write, but that has been put to bed.

Rather than text you all night long, and make you think that I care, you've made me the writer that I've always wanted to be.

Maybe you really needed space, as you're stressed out to the max. Well, I looked it up and Google did say, just to leave you be.

If you really do care like you said you do, I'll hear from you again. And if that's not meant to be, well you have made me a writer.

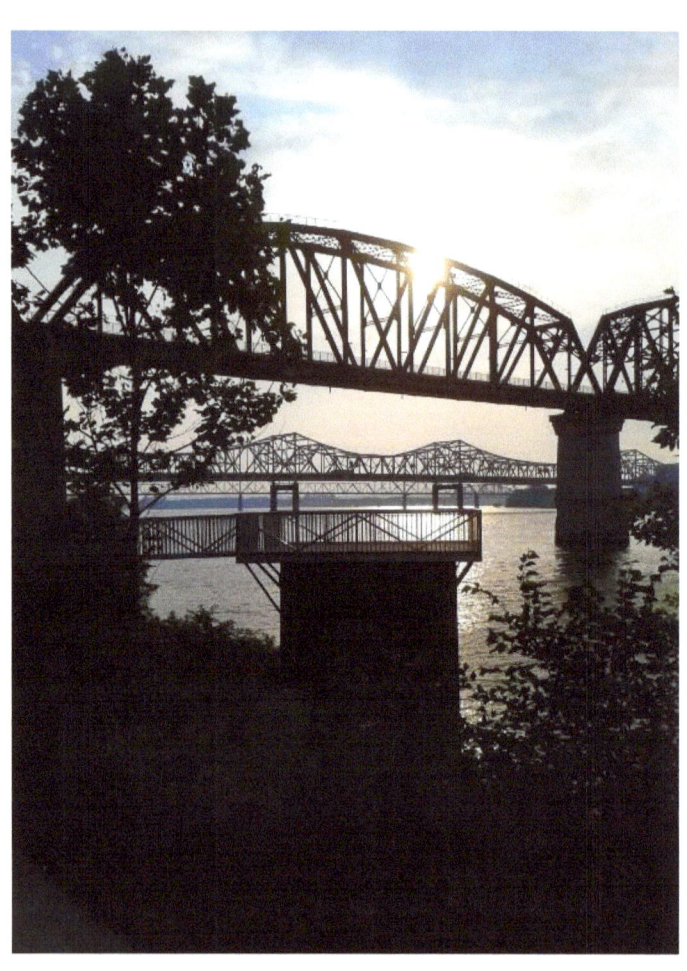

Proud and Prolific

I've become somewhat prolific, in my writing overnight. It beats the need to text my sweet and it makes me oh so proud.

Maybe now I can publish my works and be someone who is: proud and prolific.

It beats the blank page of writer's block, but man I need some sleep. I've gotta keep this day job till my writing gets me on my feet, and I'm proud and prolific.

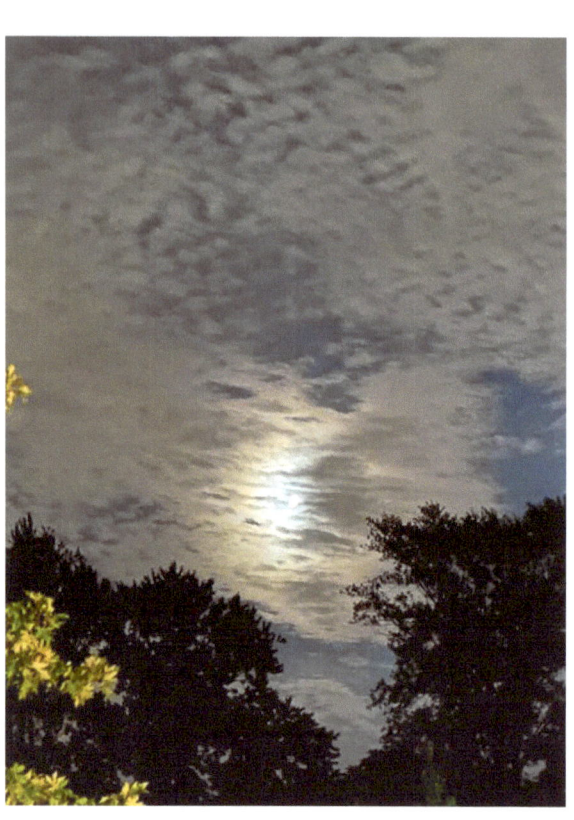

When You Love a Phantom

It was love at first sight; this most definitely is true. Although in the six months since, I've seen not a clue… He says that he loves me but hide nor hair and all that jazz.

It's a phone call here, and a text there. Most often it's a couple of months and then out of nowhere. Is this what it's like to date a Navy Seal? I assure you there's no pizzazz.

Taken for granted? Not yes, but not no. There are things that I know that I'm not sure if I should. If trust is what we're talking about here, how can it be earned when there's so much to fear?

The excitement of the anticipation. Then the downtrodden trepidation. The hope and contentment of having that spark, then I'm just left here in the dark!

This I think is what it's like, when you love a phantom.

THE END

www.ingramcontent.com/pod-product-compliance
Lightning Source LLC
Chambersburg PA
CBHW040258220526
45473CB00002B/525